THE OFFICIAL GAME GUIDE TO STAR WARS HUNTERS AND WALKTHROUGH

Step-by-step guide to upgrading characters with weapons, abilities, and cosmetics to gain the edge

Ryan W. Perez

Star wars hunters

Intentionally left blank

Copyright © Ryan W. Perez, 2024

DISCLAIMER

This book, "THE OFFICIAL GAME GUIDE TO STAR WARS HUNTERS AND WALKTHROUGH" is an unofficial guide and is not endorsed by or affiliated with the creators or original copyright holders of "Star wars hunters".

The strategies, tips, and secrets discussed in this guide are the author's interpretations and personal insights into the game and are intended to help enhance the gaming experience for players.

Table of Contents

INTRODUCTION 7
PART 1: WELCOME TO THE HUNTING GROUNDS 11
CHAPTER 1 12
Introduction to Star Wars Hunters 12
CHAPTER 2 22
Mastering the Basics 22
CHAPTER 3 32
Hunters' Gallery - Unveiling the Legends of the
Arena 32
PART 2 39
THE ART OF THE HUNT 39
CHAPTER 4 40
Upgrading Your Hunters - Sharpening Your Tools for
Victory 40
CHAPTER 5 53
Weapon Workshop - Forging Instruments of Fury 53
CHAPTER 6 63
Powering Up Abilities - Unleashing the Force Within
63
CHAPTER 7 72
The Look of a Champion - Expressing Yourself on
the Hunting Grounds 72
PART 3 82

ADVANCED HUNTING TECHNIQUES   82

CHAPTER 8   83

Mastering the Arena - From Novice to Legendary Hunter   83

CONCLUSION   92

PART 4   96

APPENDICES & RESOURCES   96

INTRODUCTION

This is the definitive resource for gamers who are looking to conquer the battlefields of this fascinating multiplayer online battle arena (MOBA) game, and we would like to take this opportunity to welcome you to the official game guide for Star Wars: Hunters. This book is the key to uncovering the mysteries of Star Wars: Hunters, and if you are a lover of the Star Wars saga and a gamer who is eager to enhance your abilities, you should read it.

In the following pages, we will guide you through the game in a step-by-step manner, giving you with expert advice, methods, and tips that will assist you in enhancing your characters with the most potent weapons, skills, and cosmetics. In order to help you achieve success in this fast-paced and competitive game, our thorough guide is meant to assist you in gaining the advantage you need.

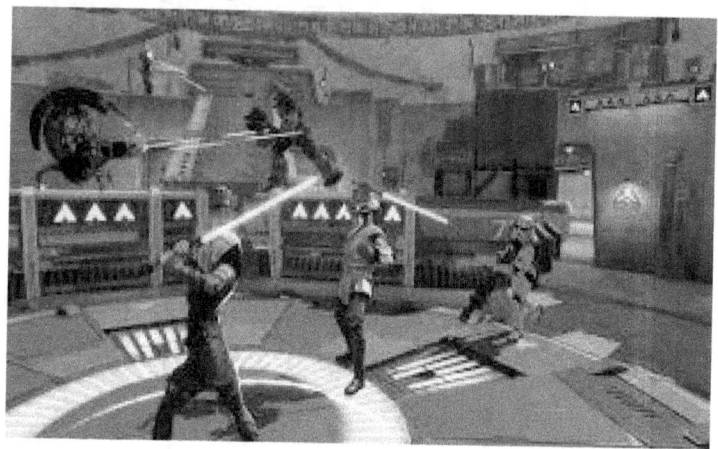

As you engage in fierce four-on-four encounters with other players in Star Wars: Hunters, you will go on an exciting journey through some of the most famous places in the Star Wars universe, including Tatooine and Coruscant. As you have the opportunity to choose from a wide variety of characters, each of whom have their own set of capabilities and playstyles, you will need to become proficient in your abilities and learn how to collaborate with your colleagues in order to achieve success.

The following are some of the important details that are included in our guide:

Character profiles and tactics, instructions to weapons and abilities, cosmetic upgrades and customization choices, and more
Tips for ranked matches and casual play, as well as strategies for special events and game modes, are included in the following: - Maps and battle arena strategies

Our guide is intended to assist you in improving your gaming and enhancing your entire experience with Star Wars: Hunters, regardless of whether you are an experienced gamer or new to the world of multiplayer online battle arenas (MOBAs). So, join us on this voyage into the universe of Star Wars: Hunters, and may the Force be with you!

In the coming chapters, we will go further into the game, studying each facet of Star Wars: Hunters and equipping you with the knowledge and abilities required to become a genuine champion. Let's get started!

PART 1: WELCOME TO THE HUNTING GROUNDS

CHAPTER 1

Introduction to Star Wars Hunters

Welcome, bounty hunter, to the wild frontier of the Outer Rim! This official guide will provide you with the knowledge to win the hunt in Star Wars Hunters, a competitive arena where cunning and strategy meet blaster fire and lightsaber fights. Whether you're a seasoned Mandalorian warrior or a young recruit fighting your way up the ranks, this complete guide will be your loyal friend.

What are Star Wars Hunters?

Star Wars Hunters takes you into the middle of a gripping tournament as bounty hunters from throughout the galaxy strive for fame, riches, and the ultimate bragging rights. Developed by Droideka Studios and set after the fall of the Empire, the game provides a unique combination of character-based hero shooting and strategic arena battle.

Imagine a colosseum overflowing with various hunters, each with their own particular battle style and equipment. Your objective? Outmaneuver, outgun, and eventually outlast your opponents to become the champion. But this is no mindless brawl. Star Wars Hunters requires mastery of your chosen character, tactical awareness, and the ability to adapt to the ever-shifting tide of combat.

Game Modes and Objectives

Star Wars Hunters has a multitude of game modes, each giving a new take on the basic competitive experience. Here's a rundown of the major modes you'll encounter:

Hunt: This free-for-all mayhem throws you against seven other hunters in a wild dash for glory. Earn points by eliminating opponents and collecting bounties spread across the map. The hunter with the most points in the end reigns supreme.

Extraction: Teamwork is crucial in this mode. Squad up with three other players and work together to destroy opposing hunters and capture vital data packets. Successfully retrieve the data points with your team intact to earn victory.

Trooper Rush: In this objective-based game, you'll join up with three pals to face battle against waves of AI-controlled stormtroopers and elite adversaries. Work together to achieve goals, destroy troops effectively, and eventually beat the enemy squad.

Showdown: This fast-paced battle mode is great for testing your talents against another player in a 1v1 situation. Sharpen your reflexes, master your character's talents, and emerge triumphant in this winner-takes-all clash.

As you move through the game and unlock new hunts, you'll have access to extra game types that cycle in and out on a regular basis. This offers a fresh and dynamic experience, continuously challenging you to adjust your strategy and master new characters.

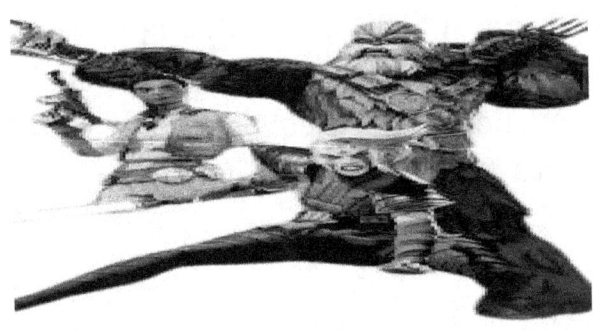

Basic Gameplay Overview

Now, let's plunge into the core of the action. Each battle in Star Wars Hunters takes place inside a defined arena on a range of classic Star Wars settings. These maps are deliberately constructed to provide various settings and strategic chances. From the blistering deserts of Tatooine to the expansive cities of Coruscant, each map poses new difficulties and tactical concerns.

You'll begin each match by picking your hunter from your roster. As you go through the game, you'll uncover a growing assortment of these distinctive characters, each with their own individual battle style, skills, and weaponry. We'll go further into character selection and customization in subsequent chapters, but for now, let's concentrate on the main gameplay loop.

Once you've chosen your hunter and entered the arena, the hunt begins! The fast-paced action revolves around movement, aiming, and utilizing your character's unique abilities. Master the art of dodging and manoeuvring to avoid enemy fire. Utilize the environment to your advantage, taking cover behind crates or using jump pads to gain a tactical position.

Weapons are a crucial aspect of Star Wars Hunters. Each hunter wields a primary weapon for sustained damage and a secondary weapon for close-quarters combat or tactical purposes. As you eliminate opponents and collect bounties scattered around the map, you'll build up your arsenal. Powerful temporary weapons like rocket launchers or sniper rifles can be picked up and unleashed for devastating effects.

But pure firepower isn't enough. Mastering your character's unique abilities is what separates a good hunter from a great one. These abilities can range from grenades and jetpack boosts to healing bursts and droid companions. Utilize them strategically to gain the upper hand, control the battlefield, and secure victory.

Remember, bounty hunters come in all shapes and sizes. Some excel at close-quarters combat, while others specialize in long-range sniping. Some are nimble and evasive, while others are heavily armored tanks. Understanding your chosen hunter's strengths and weaknesses is crucial for formulating a winning strategy.

As the match progresses, the tension mounts. Bounty pucks dropped by eliminated hunters become valuable targets, adding another layer of strategic depth. Collect these pucks to increase your score and potentially become the prime target for other hunters. The final moments of a Star Wars Hunters match are often heart-stopping affairs, demanding quick thinking, strategic positioning, and hair-trigger reflexes.

Mastering the Art of the Hunt

While basic gameplay mechanics are straightforward, becoming a dominant force in the arena requires dedication and tactical acumen. Here are some key aspects to consider for mastering the hunt:

Know Your Target: Before diving headfirst into battle, take a moment to familiarize yourself with the roster of hunters. Each possesses unique abilities, strengths, and weaknesses. Understanding these nuances will allow you to predict enemy movements, counter their attacks, and exploit their vulnerabilities.

Teamwork Makes the Dream Work: While some game modes are free-for-all battles, a significant portion of Star Wars Hunters revolves around team-based objectives. Effective communication and coordination with your teammates are paramount for success. Utilize the in-game ping system to mark targets, strategize on voice chat, and revive fallen comrades when possible.

The Power of Adaptation: The battlefields of Star Wars Hunters are dynamic and ever-changing. Be prepared to adjust your strategies on the fly. Analyze the flow of battle, identify enemy tactics, and adapt your approach accordingly. Learn to use the environment to your advantage, utilizing cover points, flanking routes, and even environmental hazards to gain the upper hand.

Practice Makes Perfect: Sharpening your skills is crucial for becoming a top-tier hunter. The game offers a dedicated practice arena where you can experiment with different characters, hone your aiming skills, and master your chosen hunter's abilities against AI opponents.

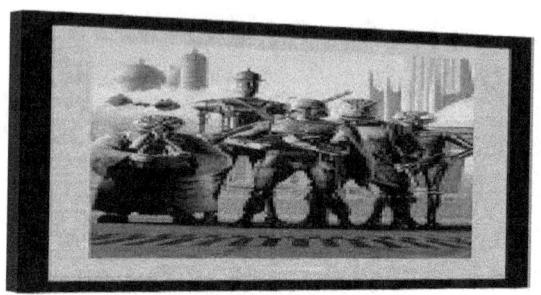

The Power of Progression: As you participate in matches and complete challenges, you'll earn experience points that level up your hunter. This unlocks new abilities, upgrades their base stats, and grants access to powerful weapon attachments. Additionally, completing daily and weekly quests rewards you with valuable resources like credits and crafting materials. These resources are essential for acquiring new hunters, customizing their appearances, and upgrading their equipment.

By mastering these core principles, you'll be well on your way to dominating the hunt. However, this is just the first step in your journey. The following chapters will delve deeper into specific aspects of the game, providing you with detailed walkthroughs, character breakdowns, strategic insights, and essential tips to customize and upgrade your hunters, giving you the edge you need to claim victory in the arena.

CHAPTER 2

Mastering the Basics

Welcome back, hunter! Now that you've learned the essential ideas of Star Wars Hunters, it's time to go deeper and develop your talents. Mastering the fundamentals of mobility, battle, and strategy is the basis upon which you'll establish your domination in the arena. This chapter will act as your instruction handbook, giving a full reference to movement controls, combat mechanics, and objective-specific methods for each game mode.

Movement and Controls

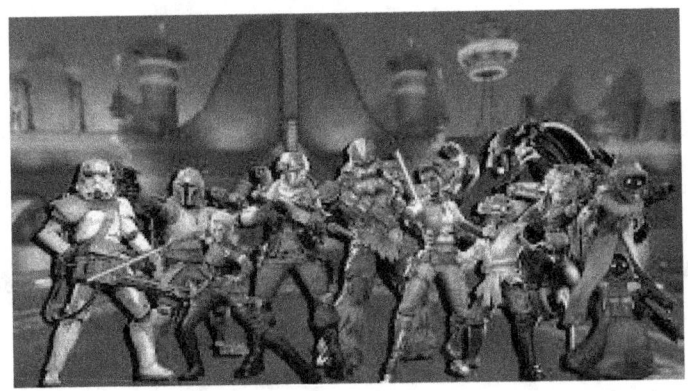

Moving with elegance and purpose is key for survival in the chaotic battlefields of Star Wars Hunters. Here's a breakdown of the basic movement controls:

Directional Pad/Analog Stick: This controls your character's movement. Utilize it to explore the surroundings, evade assaults, and strategically arrange yourself.

Jump Button: The jump button helps you to leap over barriers, scale ledges, and gain a tactical advantage by reaching higher areas. Mastering jump timing is vital for evading enemy fire and moving through difficult areas.

Dash Button: Some hunters feature a dash ability that offers a fast burst of mobility in a designated direction. Use this to evade oncoming strikes, close the distance on fleeing adversaries, or escape risky situations.

Aiming: Utilize the aiming reticle to target your opponents. Aiming down sights (ADS) with some weapons gives increased accuracy at the expense of losing some mobility.

Combat Mechanics: Aiming, Shooting, and Abilities

Beyond mobility, understanding battle techniques is the key to obtaining success. Here's a breakdown of the key aspects:

Weapons: Each hunter uses a main weapon for sustained damage, commonly a blaster rifle or a version thereof. Secondary weapons give close-quarter alternatives or tactical conveniences, such as grenades or sniper rifles.

Manage your ammunition intelligently, pick the correct weapon for the circumstances, and reload at opportune intervals.

Shooting: Shooting mechanics are simple. Aim at your target and unleash your weapons. Remember to allow for bullet travel time, particularly at vast distances. Utilize cover to prevent taking excessive damage while returning fire.

Abilities: These are unique to each hunter and give a tactical edge. Abilities may vary from attacking moves like grenades or rockets to defensive measures like shields and healing bursts. Utilize your powers wisely to get an advantage, manage the battlefield, and earn kills.

Here are some other battle tips to keep in mind:

Weak spots: Some opponents, notably elite troops and competing hunters, possess weak spots. Targeting these vulnerable places with accurate aim causes substantially more damage.

Headshots: Landing a headshot on an opposing hunter is frequently an immediate termination.

Mastering your aim and employing weapons with high headshot damage is a key skill.

Melee Attacks: While not the major emphasis, certain hunters possess lethal melee attacks for close-quarter fighting. Utilize these wisely when the chance presents itself.

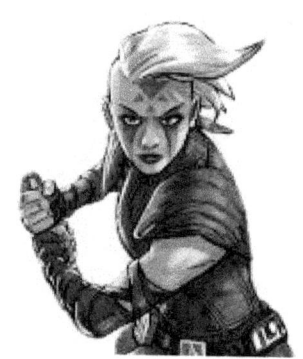

Objectives and Strategies for Different Game Modes

Now that you've perfected your mobility and fighting abilities, let's look into the unique goals and tactics for each game mode:

Hunt: This free-for-all frenzy is about survival and getting the most points. Here are some significant strategies:

Focus on eliminations: Eliminating opponents offers a substantial score increase. However, emphasize strategic battles and avoid mindlessly pursuing kills.

Collect bounties: Bounty pucks dropped by eliminated hunters provide extra points. However, be mindful of becoming a prime target by collecting too many bounties.

Control the map: Learn the map structure and leverage strategic choke points to your advantage. Utilize shelter intelligently and avoid open locations where you're exposed.

Extraction: Teamwork is crucial in this mode.

Here's how to succeed:

Communicate effectively: Coordinate with your team using voice chat or pings. Share information about enemy positions and goals.

Divide and conquer: Split your squad intelligently to secure data points while maintaining a defensive presence on the map.

Protect the carrier: The comrade carrying the data packet is a prime target. Guard them and resuscitate them if they fall.

Trooper Rush: Objective-based mayhem awaits. Here's how to dominate:

Clear waves efficiently: Work together to destroy enemy warriors fast. Utilize skills that provide AoE damage and prioritize removing harder elite adversaries.

Complete objectives: Focus on capturing points or protecting objectives as necessary by the current map. Coordinate your work and communicate efficiently.

Utilize the environment: Certain regions provide tactical benefits. Utilize cover spots and strategically positioned turrets to capture objectives and defeat opposing waves.

Showdown: This 1v1 fight challenges your sheer talent and mastery of your chosen hunter. Here's how to emerge victorious:

Know your opponent: Just as in Hunt mode, evaluating your opponent's strengths and weaknesses is vital. Analyze their hunting choices and modify your approach appropriately.

Aggressive vs. Defensive: Decide if an aggressive or defensive playstyle is best suited for your chosen hunter and the map layout. Aggressive players strive to narrow the gap and overwhelm their opponent with weapons. Defensive players concentrate on hit-and-run tactics, employing cover and clever placement to wear down their opponent.

Mind Games: Utilize smart dodges and feints to throw off your opponent's aim. Learn their assault patterns and anticipate their actions to counter successfully.

Master your abilities: This is when properly mastering your chosen hunter's talents becomes vital. Utilize your powers offensively to create opportunities and defensively to counter your opponent's assaults.

Environmental awareness: Utilize the environment to your advantage. Certain maps provide environmental threats like exploding canisters or falling debris. Learn to manage these components to obtain the upper hand.

Practice Makes Perfect

The best way to absorb these mechanics and tactics is via focused practice. Thankfully, Star Wars Hunters includes a dedicated practice arena. Here, you may experiment with different hunts, perfect your aiming abilities against AI opponents, and try out various battle strategies in a risk-free environment. Utilize the practice arena to:

Experiment with hunters: Before going into competitive battles, try out various hunters in the practice arena. This enables you to explore characters that fit your playstyle and practice their distinctive powers.

Master your aim: The practice arena is a wonderful area to develop your aiming abilities. Practice shooting at fixed and moving targets, correcting for bullet travel time, and learning aim-down-sights (ADS) mechanics.

Test out combos: Each hunter's powers may be strung together in unique ways. Utilize the practice arena to experiment with various ability combinations and uncover efficient attack and defense strategies.

Beyond the Basics

Mastering the basics is simply the first step in your road to become a renowned hunter. The next chapters will go further into certain parts of the game, including thorough analysis of each hunter, advanced battle techniques, and in-depth guidance for customizing and upgrading your characters to optimize their potential. Remember, practice, plan, and adapt - these are the foundations around which your domination in the arena will be based.

CHAPTER 3

Hunters' Gallery – Unveiling the Legends of the Arena

This chapter serves as your full reference to the current roster of hunters, including insights into their roles, playstyles, and talents.

Introduction to the Hunter Roster

Star Wars Hunters has a broad roster of characters, each with their own individual narrative, battle style, and set of powers. As you continue through the game, you'll acquire these hunters via numerous means, including completing tasks, earning credits through gaming, and even through odd fortunate drops. This chapter will offer a quick summary of each hunter, grouped by their major role: Offense, Defense, and Support.

Hunters by Role

Offense: These hunters excel in dealing heavy damage and aggressively taking down opponents. They are suited for gamers that love a fast-paced, action-oriented playstyle.

Aran Tal (Mandalorian): A descendant of an ancient Mandalorian clan, Aran Tal is a master of close-quarter fighting. He wields strong blasters and jetpack moves to overpower his adversaries.

Imara Vex (Smuggler): This crafty smuggler deploys a devastating mix of long-range guns and high-explosive devices to destroy her prey from afar.

J-3DI (Bounty Droid): This merciless droid assassin is a relentless killing machine. He boasts a varied armament of blasters, rockets, and even a self-destruct option for ultimate devastation.

Rieve (Smuggler): A charming smuggler with a propensity for explosives, Rieve deploys grenade launchers and proximity mines to sow havoc on the battlefield.

Utooni (Wookiee Warrior): This towering Wookiee warrior is a force of nature. He exploits his tremendous strength and a strong bowcaster to dominate close-quarter fights.

Defense: These hunters concentrate in absorbing harm and defending themselves and their comrades. They are perfect for those that appreciate a strategic, tank-like playstyle.

Charr (Trandoshan): This enormous Trandoshan hunter is a master of close-quarters fighting and crowd management. He wields a vibroblade and a deployable shield to dominate the front lines, absorbing hostile fire and disrupting opponent formations.

Grozz (Ugnaught): This highly armored Ugnaught exploits industrial equipment repurposed for battle. He holds a gigantic wrench and a deployable energy shield, giving him a strong defensive presence on the battlefield.

Sentinel (Imperial robot): This modified Imperial robot is a walking arsenal. It combines massive blaster guns and a deployable energy shield to hold down crucial spots and defend friends.

Slingshot (Jawa): Don't underestimate this resourceful Jawa scavenger! Slingshot wields a modified mining weapon and a deployable trash shield to hold his own against bigger opponents.

Support: These hunters give crucial aid to their allies via healing, boosts, and strategic usefulness. They are great for players that appreciate a supporting playstyle, assisting their team to win.

Skora (Zabrak Nightsister): This mysterious Zabrak wields dark Force abilities to heal friends, harm opponents, and control the battlefield with illusions.

Sprocket (Astromech Droid): This resourceful droid utilizes its tools to repair allies, disrupt enemy droids, and provide tactical buffs to his team.

Zaina (Rebel Pilot): This skilled pilot utilizes modified flight technology to provide aerial support, healing allies from above and raining down blaster fire on enemies.

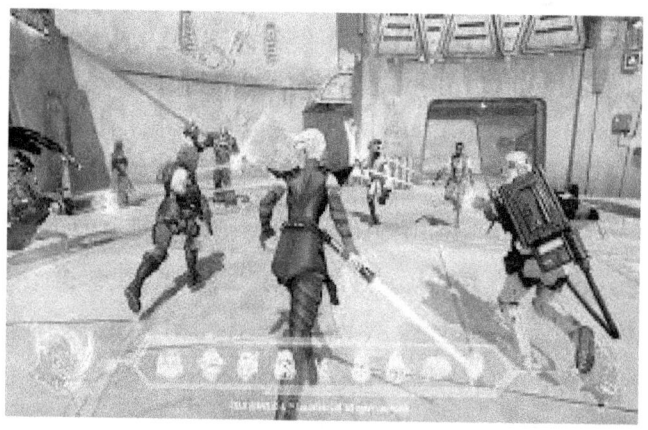

Choosing Your Starting Hunter

With a diverse roster of hunters at your disposal, choosing your starting character can be daunting. Here are some factors to consider:

Playstyle: Do you prefer to get up close and personal with a blaster rifle, or rain down fire from afar? Do you enjoy protecting your allies or unleashing devastating attacks? Identify your preferred playstyle and choose a hunter that aligns with it.

Difficulty: Some hunters are easier to learn than others. Characters like Aran Tal or Imara Vex offer a more straightforward offense-oriented approach. Hunters like Skora or Sprocket require a deeper understanding of their support abilities.

Practice: Don't hesitate to experiment! The practice arena is a great place to test out different hunters and discover which one best suits your skills and preferences.

Remember, there's no single "best" hunter. The optimal choice depends on your individual playstyle, team composition, and the specific game mode you're tackling. As you progress and unlock more hunters, you'll develop a mastery of diverse characters, allowing you to adapt your strategy to any situation.

The next chapters will delve deeper into each hunter, providing detailed breakdowns of their abilities, recommended upgrades, and strategic tips for maximizing their effectiveness on the battlefield. With this knowledge, you'll be well-equipped to choose the right hunter for the job and dominate the competition in Star Wars Hunters!

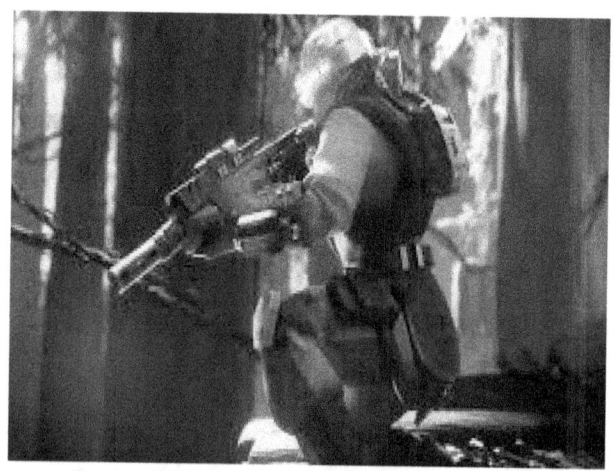

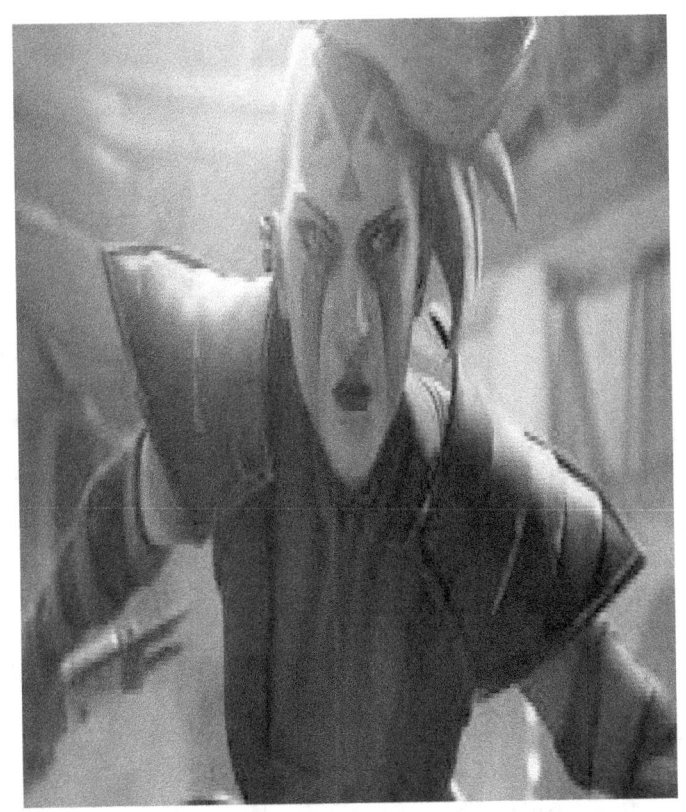

PART 2

THE ART OF THE HUNT

CHAPTER 4

Upgrading Your Hunters – Sharpening Your Tools for Victory

Welcome back, hunter! Now that you've explored the vast pool of characters and perfected your battle abilities, it's time to dig into the realm of customization and upgrades. This chapter serves as your one-stop guide to boosting your hunter's potential with clever upgrades, strong weapon attachments, and beautiful cosmetics.

Earning the Means to Upgrade

Star Wars Hunters provides a range of materials that fuel your hunter's development. Here's a rundown of the major currencies you'll encounter:

Credits: The major money used to acquire new hunters, enhance abilities, and build weapon attachments. You may earn credits via several ways, including finishing matches, engaging in daily and weekly tasks, and collecting prizes from the season pass.

Crafting Materials: These specialized materials are used to construct strong weapon attachments that boost your hunter's firepower and usefulness. Crafting materials are generally earned via deconstructing undesirable gear and partaking in particular challenges.

Weapon and Ability Upgrades: Impact and Strategies

Each hunter carries distinct weapons and skills. By spending in-game credits, you may acquire enhancements for these essential features of your character. Here's how these improvements work:

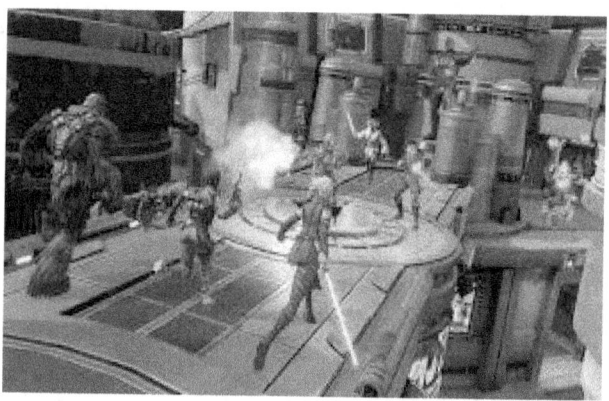

Weapon Upgrades: These improvements concentrate on enhancing the operation and effectiveness of your hunter's main and secondary weapons. Examples include expanded magazine size, better firing rate, and higher damage output.

Ability Upgrades: These upgrades unlock extra functionality and intensify the impact of your hunter's skills. For instance, an ability upgrade might boost healing efficacy, lengthen the duration of a buff, or offer an extra effect to a special strike.

Upgrading Strategies:

With a vast selection of improvement choices available, deciding where to put your cash is vital. Here are some strategies to consider:

Focus on Your Main: Don't stretch yourself thin! While experimenting with various hunts is encouraged, prioritize improving the character you use most often. This guarantees you optimize the return on your investment.
Target Core Upgrades First: Upgrades that strengthen your hunter's fundamental stats, like higher health or enhanced movement speed, are frequently a solid pick. These basic

enhancements boost all elements of your gaming.

Tailor to Your Playstyle: Do you prefer a more aggressive approach? Focus on weapon upgrades that boost your damage output. Favor a supporting role? Prioritize upgrades that increase the efficacy of your healing or buffing skills.

Utilize Practice Arena: The practice arena is an important tool for trying out various upgrade combinations. Experiment and observe how particular improvements impact your hunter's performance before committing resources permanently.

Introduction to Cosmetics and Customization

While boosting your hunter's fighting efficiency is critical, displaying your uniqueness is also important. Star Wars Hunters provides a wealth of cosmetic modification choices to customize your characters:

Hunter Skins: These skins modify the look of your hunter, enabling you to obtain new clothes and armor sets that express your distinctive taste. Weapon Wraps: Change the visual look of your hunter's weapons, giving a bit of flare to your armory.

Emotes and Victory postures: Express your domination (or displeasure) with a range of emotes and victory postures. These are mainly decorative but offer a layer of individuality to your gaming experience.

Earning Cosmetics:

Cosmetics may be acquired by numerous methods:

Direct buy: Use your hard-earned credits to buy particular cosmetic items from the in-game shop. Season Pass prizes: The seasonal progression system delivers distinctive cosmetic prizes as you level up your season pass.

Limited-Time Events: Participate in special events to unlock unique and exclusive cosmetic items.

Beyond the Upgrades

Upgrading your hunters and customizing their look are essential milestones in your road to become a famous bounty hunter. However, the ultimate mastery rests in combining these advantages with your polished talents and tactical brilliance.

Advanced Upgrading Techniques: Crafting and Optimization

While basic improvements give a good foundation, unlocking your hunter's potential demands going into the realm of crafting and min-maxing. Here's how to take your enhancements to the next level:

Crafting Weapon Attachments: Crafting resources enable you to manufacture strong weapon attachments that dramatically boost your hunter's firepower and usefulness. Weapon attachments give a number of bonuses, including:

Increased Damage: Enhance your raw damage output for a more aggressive playstyle.

Improved Accuracy: Reduce recoil and bullet spread for pinpoint accuracy.

Faster Reload Speeds: Get back into the battle faster with shorter reload times.

Elemental Effects: Attach elemental modifiers like fire or cold to inflict extra damage kinds and status effects on foes.

Dismantling Gear: Don't be scared to destroy unneeded gear! This technique salvages manufacturing components from unneeded weapons and attachments, enabling you to manufacture the improvements you actually need.

Optimizing Your Upgrades:

Not all improvements are made equal. Here are some techniques to guarantee you get the most out of your resources:

Synergy is Key: Consider how your improvements function together. Focus on combinations that compliment one other and boost your overall playstyle. For example, matching a damage-boosting upgrade with a weapon attachment that boosts firing rate generates a tremendous offensive synergy.

Rare vs. Common Gear: While higher-rarity gear (Epic and Legendary) delivers more substantial stat bonuses, getting them might be more tough. Don't underestimate the usefulness of well-upgraded common gear, particularly in the early phases of the game.

experimenting is Crucial: The best way to uncover the ideal upgrading route for your selected hunter is via experimenting. Utilize the practice arena to try out various combos and observe how they affect your gameplay.

The Power of Sets

Many hunters feature distinct "set bonuses" that give extra rewards while donning various combinations of gear. These set boosts may dramatically increase your hunter's powers and playstyle. Here's how to exploit them effectively:

Determine Set Bonuses: Review the description of each piece of gear to determine any connected set bonuses. Look for items that belong to the same set and equip them together to trigger the bonus.

Tailor to Your Needs: Choose set bonuses that match your playstyle. For example, a set bonus that boosts healing received could be great for a support-oriented hunter, while a bonus that amplifies critical damage might suit an offensive powerhouse.

Balancing Act: While set bonuses are strong, don't forgo key improvements for the sake of triggering a bonus. Maintain a balance between set benefits and individual upgrade efficacy.

The Art of Min-Maxing

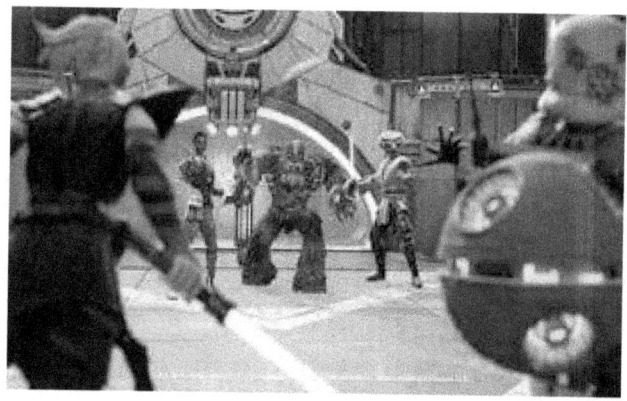

Min-maxing refers to the process of maximizing your character for certain strengths while reducing shortcomings. This may be a complicated procedure, but for determined players, it can offer major results:

Understanding metrics: Familiarize yourself with the many metrics that determine your hunter's effectiveness, including health, damage output, ability cooldown, and critical hit probability.

Prioritize attributes: Identify which attributes are most critical for your selected hunter and playstyle. Focus your improvements on optimizing these essential attributes while ensuring other parts stay functioning.

Data Analysis: Advanced players may employ in-game data and post-match reports to find areas for growth. Analyze your performance statistics and decide which improvements will solve your deficiencies most effectively.

Conclusion

Upgrading your hunters is a process, not a destination. As you move through the game, gain new gear, and experiment with alternative techniques, your knowledge of upgrades and their influence will grow. By employing the facts and methods offered in this chapter, you'll be well on your way to building the perfect hunter, a force to be reckoned with in the arenas of Star Wars Hunters! ,

CHAPTER 5

Weapon Workshop – Forging Instruments of Fury

This chapter serves as your specialized weapon workshop, giving a full reference to weapon kinds, upgrade tactics, and the art of finding the best weapon for your chosen hunter.

Weapon Tiers and Rarity

The armoury of Star Wars Hunters includes a broad selection of weapons, each with its individual strengths and limitations. Weapons are defined by two important factors: Tier and Rarity.

Tier: Weapons are classed by tiers, with higher tiers typically having improved basic stats and possibly more powerful upgrade choices. These levels are generally indicated by color:

Common (White): These basic weapons are easily accessible and provide a great basis for beginner players.

Uncommon (Green): These weapons provide a minor upgrade over common weapons, offering a solid mix between accessibility and effectiveness.

Rare (Blue): These mid-tier weapons give large stat enhancements and open more sophisticated upgrading possibilities.

Epic (Purple): These formidable weapons have amazing basic stats and allow access to the most effective upgrade options.

Legendary (Gold): The pinnacle of weapon technology, these legendary weapons provide unrivalled power and unique upgrade pathways that may radically change their utility.

Rarity: Rarity further separates weapons within a tier. larger rarity weapons often hold somewhat better basic stats and have a larger probability of rolling desired upgrade modifications.

Weapon Stats: The Nuts and Bolts of Ballistics

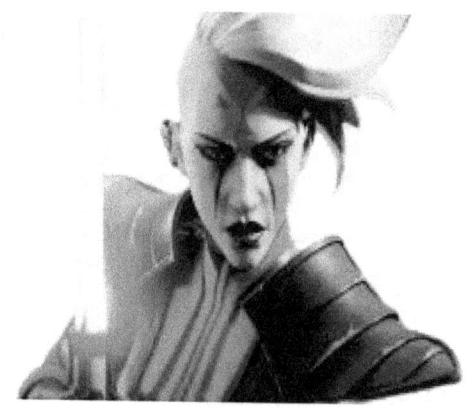

Beyond tier and rarity, knowing the key metrics that determine a weapon's performance is vital. Here's a summary of the important metrics you'll encounter:

Damage: This stat governs the sheer power of your weapon, determining the number of health points lost from your enemy with each hit.

Range: This characteristic affects the effective distance at which your weapon may deal damage. Weapons with greater range excel in sniping and long-distance confrontations, while those with lower range are better suitable for close-quarter fighting.

Fire Rate: This rating represents the rate at which your weapon can launch projectiles. Weapons with a fast firing rate may release a quick torrent of fire, while those with a slower fire rate need more accurate targeting and timing.

Reload Speed: This attribute governs the time it takes to reload your weapon once it has exhausted its ammo. Faster reload times are critical for sustaining constant damage output.

Clip Size: This characteristic reflects the amount of rounds your weapon can fire before needing a reload. Larger clip sizes enable for continuous shooting, whereas lower clip sizes need more frequent reloading.

Accuracy: This characteristic determines the spread of your weapon's projectiles. Higher accuracy results in tighter groups of shots, while lesser accuracy leads to a broader spread, making it more tough to strike targets at long range.

Upgrading Weapon Stats: Sharpening Your Tools

Each weapon contains upgrade slots that enable you to further tailor its performance. These upgrades strengthen the fundamental attributes indicated above, enabling you to personalize your weapon to your individual requirements and playstyle. Here are some upgrading considerations:

Balancing for Synergy: Upgrades frequently affect numerous stats concurrently. For instance, an improvement can boost damage but somewhat reduce accuracy. Consider how these adjustments synergize with your general playstyle and the skills of your selected hunter.

Specialization vs. Versatility: Do you prefer a weapon that specializes in one area, such boosting damage output for a sniper build? Or do you want a more adaptable weapon with balanced stats appropriate for diverse situations? Decide on your strategy and select enhancements that match your choice.

Hunter Synergy: Consider how your weapon improvements match your hunter's talents. For example, if a hunter possessed a great close-range strike, improving a weapon for enhanced damage at close quarters might make a deadly offensive combo.

Choosing the Right Weapon for Your Hunter

With a large arsenal at your disposal, finding the best weapon for your hunter might be overwhelming. Here are some points to bear in mind:

Hunter Role: Consider your hunter's major role (offense, defense, support). Offensive hunters often benefit from weapons with high damage output and firing rate, while defensive hunters could choose guns with greater range and precision. Support hunters could pick weapons with utility features, such as area-of-effect damage or status effects.

Playstyle: Are you a lover of fierce, close-quarter combat? Opt for guns with high damage and firing rate. Do you prefer a more strategic, long-range approach? Choose weapons with higher range and accuracy.

Ultimately, the greatest weapon is the one that compliments your playstyle and enables you to optimize your efficiency on the battlefield.

Map Considerations: Certain maps favor various weapon types. Open maps with vast sightlines encourage the usage of long-range rifles, whereas close-quartered maps benefit from shotguns and high-damage pistols. Adapt your weapon choice depending on the map you're playing on.

Advanced Weapon Techniques

Beyond basic stats and upgrades, knowing several extra weapon mechanics may substantially boost your performance. Here are some advanced approaches to explore:

Critical Hits: Certain weapons have a chance to score critical hits, delivering much greater damage. Upgrades and focusing at certain weak places on adversaries will enhance your critical hit probability.

Headshots: Landing a headshot on an opposing hunter generally leads to an immediate elimination. Mastering your aim and deploying weapons with great precision are vital for boosting headshot potential.

Elemental Effects: Some weapons cause elemental damage, such as fire or cold. These effects may cause more damage over time and can hamper opponent mobility. Choosing the proper elemental damage type for various scenarios might offer you an advantage.

Weapon Experimentation is Key

The greatest way to find the right weapon for your hunter is via testing. Here are some tips:

Utilize the Practice Arena: The practice arena enables you to try out various weapon kinds and upgrade combinations without losing your progress in actual battles. Experiment with different weapons and experience how they feel in your hands.

Observe Successful Players: Watch replays of skilled players that deploy the same hunter as you. Analyze their weapon selections and upgrading tactics to gather useful information.

Adapt and Evolve: As you perfect your abilities and move through the game, your weapon choices could alter. Don't be scared to experiment and change your arsenal depending on your developing demands.

The Power of Choice

Your weapon is an extension of yourself in the arenas. Choosing the appropriate one and learning its subtleties is important for success. By studying weapon tiers, stats, and upgrade options, you'll be well-equipped to construct the ideal arsenal, a lethal instrument that will strike terror into the hearts of your opponents. The future chapters will go further into certain hunts, including suggested weapon loadouts and strategic ideas for conquering the battlefield with each distinct character. Remember, a competent hunter with the correct weapon is a force to be reckoned with. Now, go out and conquer the arenas!

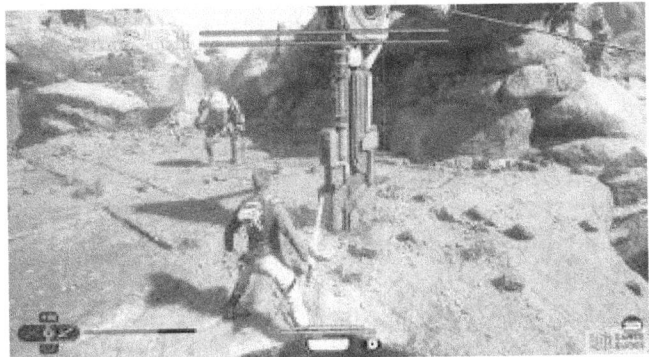

CHAPTER 6

Powering Up Abilities – Unleashing the Force Within

Welcome back, hunter! Having mastered your weapons and perfected your fighting skills, it's time to dig into the core of your hunter's strength - their unique talents. This chapter provides a full guide to understanding skills, improving their efficiency, and building devastating synergy that will dominate the battlefield.

Ability Types and Effects: A Spectrum of Power

Each hunter boasts a specific set of talents that determine their playstyle and fighting capability. These skills may be roughly divided into three groups:

Offensive skills: These skills are meant to inflict direct harm on your opponent or restrict their mobility and effectiveness. Examples include explosives, rocket barrages, and forceful melee blows. Offensive talents are vital for aggressive hunters who strive to remove adversaries with deadly power.

Defensive skills: These skills concentrate on defending yourself and your teammates from damage. Examples include shields, healing bursts, and deployable cover. Defensive talents are vital for support hunters who emphasize keeping their squad alive and in the battle.

Utility Abilities: These abilities provide a variety of tactical advantages beyond direct harm or protection. Examples include speed enhancements, area-of-effect stuns, and temporary invisibility. Utility abilities may be employed for many reasons, from starting surprise assaults to controlling opponent movement and securing strategic goals.

Understanding Ability Effects

Beyond their core damaging or support roles, abilities typically feature extra effects that may greatly alter your gameplay. Here are some major ability impacts to consider:

Cooldown Timers: Each ability has a cooldown period that specifies the time it takes for the ability to recharge after being used. Managing your cooldowns efficiently is vital for keeping a continual flow of tactical choices in combat.

region of Effect (AoE): Some abilities effect a defined region surrounding the hunter, hurting or boosting several foes or allies within range. Understanding the AoE of your skills enables you to optimize their influence on the battlefield.

Status affects: Certain skills may inflict status affects on adversaries, such as delaying their mobility, lowering their damage output, or even blinding them briefly. Utilizing status affects intelligently may offer you a major edge in battle.

Synergy with Weapons: Some abilities may synergize with particular weapon kinds or upgrades. For example, an ability that improves critical hit probability would work especially well with a high-accuracy sniper rifle. Explore these synergies to unleash deadly combinations.

Upgrading Ability Levels: Unlocking New Potential

By investing in-game credits, you may raise the level of your hunter's talents. Upgrading abilities often brings numerous benefits:

Increased Effectiveness: The main impact of an ability, such as damage output for an offensive ability or healing potency for a defensive ability, frequently rises as you upgrade its level.

Enhanced Effects: Upgrading abilities might unlock extra features and effects. For instance, an enhanced stun ability can lock foes in place for a longer time.

Reduced Cooldown: Certain ability improvements lessen the cooldown timeframe, enabling you to utilize the ability more often in combat.

Prioritizing Upgrades: Strategies for Efficiency

With many talents at your disposal, deciding which upgrades to spend in is vital. Here are some techniques to optimize the return on your resources:

Focus on Core skills: Every hunter boasts a core set of skills that determine their playstyle. Prioritize improving these basic talents to unleash their full potential.

Complement Your Playstyle: Do you like a playstyle based on aggressive damage dealing? Focus on strengthening offensive powers. Do you love supporting your squad with heels and buffs? Upgrade your support abilities first.

Addressing Weaknesses: If you find yourself lacking in a certain area, try improving skills that target that shortcoming. For example, if trying to live, prioritize defensive ability improvements.

Creating Effective Ability Synergies

The ultimate power of your skills resides not in their separate strength, but in how you link them together to produce deadly combinations. Here's how to access the power of synergy:

Identify Combos: Experiment in the practice arena to see how your talents may be strung together for optimum impact. For instance, a hunter may employ a movement-boosting ability to narrow the gap on an adversary, followed by a strong melee assault.

Ability Order Matters: The order in which you utilize your skills may dramatically affect the efficiency of your combinations. Experiment to determine the ideal sequence for maximum damage output, usefulness, or survival.

Synergy with Hunter Kit: Consider how your talents synergize with your hunter's other assets, such as weapons and passive skills. For instance, an ability that improves critical hit probability can be exceptionally potent when used in combination with a weapon with a high critical hit rate.

Advanced Ability Tactics

Beyond fundamental combinations, understanding several advanced ability methods may improve your gaming to the next level:

Predictive Casting: Anticipate your opponent's moves and cast abilities appropriately. For instance, knowing an enemy's dodge roll might enable you to pre-emptively position a destructive AoE ability in their path.

Combo cancelling: Certain advanced tactics include cancelling an ability animation prematurely to trigger the following ability in the sequence quicker. Mastering combo cancelling may substantially boost the speed and fluidity of your battle actions.

Environmental Awareness: Utilize the environment to boost your talents. For instance, utilizing a shield ability near explosive canisters might possibly generate a deadly explosion that affects both you and your attacker (use with care!).

Practice Makes Perfect

The practice area is an excellent tool for developing your talents. Here are some methods to apply it effectively:

Experiment with Combos: Test out various ability combinations to determine the most efficient sequences for your selected hunter.

Practice Timing: Refine your timing using abilities that have particular durations or demand exact activation times.

Counter Strategies: Practice utilizing your talents to counter those of other hunters. For instance, learn how to avoid or stop opposing abilities with your own.

Conclusion

Your talents are an important element of your hunter's arsenal, giving numerous tactical choices and powerful offensive or supporting capabilities. By knowing various skill types, increasing their efficacy via upgrades, and mastering the art of chaining them together into explosive combinations, you'll be well on your way to conquering your adversaries in the arenas. The following chapters will go further into certain hunters, offering thorough analysis of their unique powers, displaying suggested ability upgrade routes, and recommending strong ability combinations to unleash upon your opponents. Remember, a trained hunter with a grasp of their powers is a very powerful force. Now, go out and explore, perfect your talents, and become a master of battle.

CHAPTER 7

The Look of a Champion - Expressing Yourself on the Hunting Grounds

Welcome back, hunter! Having polished your fighting skills, perfected your gear, and unleashed destructive powers, it's time to shift your focus to the domain of aesthetics. This chapter goes into the realm of cosmetic modification in Star Wars Hunters, enabling you to express your uniqueness and strike terror (or maybe laughter) into the hearts of your opponents with flair.

A Galaxy of Style: Cosmetic Customization Options

Star Wars Hunters provides a wealth of cosmetic choices to customize your hunters and exhibit your individual style. Here's an overview of the primary customization categories:

Hunter Skins: These modify the look of your hunter, enabling you to acquire and wear various clothes and armour sets that represent your particular taste. Hunter skins may vary from elegant and futuristic to rough and battle-worn, allowing a multitude of thematic possibilities.

Weapon Wraps: Change the visual look of your hunter's weapons, giving a bit of flare to your armoury. Weapon wraps may flaunt diverse colors, textures, and even thematic patterns to complement your hunter's overall design.

Emotes and Victory Poses: Express your domination (or annoyance) with a range of emotes and victory postures. These are mainly decorative but offer a layer of individuality to your gaming experience. Imagine insulting a vanquished opponent with a joyful victory posture or making a polite bow after a tight fight.

The Road to Looking Legendary: Earning Cosmetics

There are multiple methods to gain the different fascinating cosmetics Star Wars Hunters offers:

Direct buy: Use your hard-earned credits to buy particular cosmetic items from the in-game shop. The shop often changes its inventory, so keep a look out for things that fit your style.

Season Pass prizes: The seasonal progression system delivers distinctive cosmetic prizes as you level up your season pass. By playing in matches and completing tasks, you'll acquire additional skins, weapon wraps, and emotes to personalize your hunter.

Limited-Time Events: Special events typically reward gamers with unique cosmetic goods for participating and accomplishing event goals. These events give a chance to get unique and special cosmetic items that set you different from the crowd.

Free Rewards: Some basic cosmetic choices are available for free upon unlocking new hunts or hitting specified milestones in the game. These basic selections give a basis for constructing your own style.

Equipping Your Style

Once you've gathered a collection of cosmetics, equipping them is a breeze:

Hunter pick Screen: From the main menu, browse to the Hunters tab and pick the hunter you desire to personalize.

Customization Menu: Within the hunter selection screen, find the "Customize" button. This displays the customization screen, presenting all possible cosmetic choices for your selected hunter.

Equipping Items: Simply choose the appropriate skin, weapon wrap, emote, or victory posture from the menu. Equipped goods will be shown on your hunter preview model.

Showcasing Your Style: With your customized appearance complete, dominate the battlefield and strike terror (or maybe amusement) into your opponents with your distinctive flair!

Making a Statement: The Power of Personalization

Cosmetic customisation goes beyond simple aesthetics. Here's how displaying your uniqueness may boost your gaming experience:

Morale enhance: Sporting a great new skin or a showy victory pose will enhance your confidence and battle spirit. Feeling comfortable about your looks might transfer into greater gaming.

Intimidation Factor: A terrifyingly-clad hunter with a threatening emote could strike dread into the hearts of certain opponents, giving you a psychological advantage.

Team Spirit: Coordinate your cosmetics with your colleagues to create a unified and visually attractive team style. Strike dread into your opponents not only with your talents, but with your cohesive and elegant presence.

The Art of Self-Expression

Star Wars Hunters gives a huge canvas for your creations. Here are some suggestions to release your inner fashionista:

Mix & Match: Experiment with various combinations of skins, weapon wraps, and emotes to create unique appearances that represent your personality. Don't be scared to break the mold and develop something genuinely distinctive.

Thematic Customization: Build your hunter's appearance around a certain theme. For instance, build a sleek and minimalist bounty hunter, a rough and battle-hardened warrior, or a flashy and showboating winner.

Seasonal Inspiration: Seasonal events typically feature thematically-inspired cosmetics. Embrace the current topic and design a look that represents the spirit of the season.

The Power of Community:

The Star Wars Hunters community focuses on self-expression and friendly rivalry. Here are several methods to share your style with others:

Social capabilities: Utilize the in-game social capabilities to exhibit your hunter's style to friends and opponents alike. Strike a stance before a match or show off your victory dance after a hard-fought fight.

Community Hubs: Engage with other players via online forums and social media groups devoted to Star Wars Hunters. Share screenshots of your personalized hunts, debate fashion trends, and encourage others with your ingenuity.

Friendly Competition: Organize friendly matches with your other hunters and flaunt your distinctive appearance while fighting it out in a spirit of friendship.

The Evolving Fashion Frontier

The universe of cosmetics in Star Wars Hunters is continually developing. Here's what to expect:

Regular Updates: New hunter skins, weapon wraps, emotes, and victory postures are routinely released to the game, giving you with even more opportunities to customize your hunter.

Limited-Edition Collaborations: Keep a watch out for unusual collaborations with other Star Wars concepts or businesses, delivering rare and highly sought-after cosmetic goods.

Community-Driven Influence: The Star Wars Hunters development team regularly considers player comments and requests when building new cosmetic choices. Make your voice known and contribute to the ever-evolving fashion scene of the game.

The Final Touch: A Word on Completionism

While getting every cosmetic item in the game might be a laudable objective, remember to emphasize pleasure and enjoyment above all else. Focus on purchasing things that actually connect with your style and improve your gaming experience. However, the excitement of the chase for that elusive limited-edition skin may be a strong motivation, so don't hesitate to participate in events and challenges if completionism is your calling!

The Look of a Champion

By embracing the realm of cosmetic modification, you'll not only show your uniqueness but also enrich your entire Star Wars Hunters experience. With a customized hunter that embodies your style and character, you'll conquer the battlefield not only with your abilities, but with your unmistakable presence. So, go out, explore, and become a famous not only for your battle skill, but for your renowned dress sense! The following chapters will go further into certain hunters, presenting graphics displaying numerous customization choices. Remember, a fashionable hunter is a confident hunter, and a confident hunter is a force to be reckoned with.

Conclusion

Cosmetic modification is crucial to expressing oneself as a hunter in Star Wars Hunters. Whether you desire a terrifying visage, a fashionable swagger, or just a personal touch, the huge number of cosmetic choices enables you to build a style that's entirely yours. Remember, a well-equipped hunter is a deadly opponent, but a well-equipped and elegant hunter is really remembered.

PART 3

ADVANCED HUNTING TECHNIQUES

CHAPTER 8

Mastering the Arena – From Novice to Legendary Hunter

Welcome back, hunter! Having polished your talents, tailored your style, and equipped yourself with the right armament, it's time to enter into the heart of the action - the arena. This chapter digs into the area of sophisticated fighting tactics, strategic placement, and the art of collaboration, converting you from a fledgling hunter into a genuinely dominating force.

Beyond Basic Combat: Advanced Tactics for the Discerning Hunter

Mastering the foundations of fighting is vital, but to fully thrive in the arenas, you need to improve your tactical awareness and create advanced plans. Here are some essential topics to concentrate on:

Understanding Opponent Hunters: Take the time to research the various hunters accessible in the game. Familiarize yourself with their strengths, weaknesses, abilities, and weapon ranges. Knowing what to expect from your opponents will help you to predict their actions and counter their methods successfully.

Environmental Awareness: The arenas are not just battlefields; they are sophisticated settings loaded with opportunity for strategic manoeuvring. Utilize cover intelligently, exploit natural dangers, and take advantage of high ground to get an edge over your opponents.

Flanking and Pincer Manoeuvres: Don't always engage head-on. Learn to flank your foes, hitting from unexpected angles to break their formations and increase your damage output. Coordinate flanking tactics with colleagues for lethal pincer strikes.

Baiting and Countering: Lure your opponents into traps by deploying faked retreats or cleverly positioned explosives. Learn to recognize and neutralize adversary skills by predicting their movements and responding rapidly with your own defensive moves.

The Art of Cover: Your Shield from Harm

The arenas feature a range of ambient items that may be employed as cover, sheltering you from opposing fire and enabling you to recover health. Here's how to employ cover effectively:

Choosing the Right Cover: Not every cover is made equal. Prioritize robust buildings that can sustain substantial damage and give complete protection from hostile fire. Avoid flimsy coverings that may be quickly ruined or give minimal protection.

Peeking and Popping: Don't stay glued to cover! Learn to peek out briefly to shoot at foes, then flee back to shelter before they can respond. This "peek-and-pop" strategy enables you to do damage while reducing your exposure to hostile fire.

Moving Between Cover: Don't become a sitting duck! Constantly move between various cover locations to avoid typical patterns and make oneself a more tough target. Utilize mobility talents to rapidly reposition oneself and keep the element of surprise.

Positioning for Domination: Mastering the Battlefield

Your location on the battlefield has a big influence on your efficacy. Here are some significant positioning tactics to consider:

High Ground Advantage: Whenever feasible, aim to secure the high ground. This gives you with a greater vision of the battlefield, enabling you to rain down fire on unsuspecting adversaries, and offers a tactical escape route if required.

Strategic Use of Objectives: In objective-based game variants, prioritize controlling crucial places like capture points or power centers. These sites typically provide strategic benefits and may swing the tide of combat in your favor.

Map Knowledge is Power: Familiarize yourself with the layout of each arena. Learn where the greatest cover locations are situated, predict enemy flanking paths, and find strategic choke points where you can hold your position or unleash deadly ambushes.

United We Stand: Teamwork and Coordination in Multiplayer Modes

Star Wars Hunters is not a single endeavour; it's a team effort. Here are some ways for enhancing collaboration and coordination with your fellow hunters:

Communication is Key: Utilize the in-game communication system to communicate information, plan assaults, and warn your teammates of incoming dangers. Clear and precise communication is crucial for effective team movements.

Understanding Roles: Recognize the strengths and limitations of your selected hunter and your teammates. Support players should concentrate healing and boosting teammates, while offensive players should focus on inflicting damage and destroying opponent threats.

Synergy and Combos: Combine the skills of your hunter with those of your teammates to generate lethal synergies and combinations. For instance, a support player's healing aura might allow an offensive player to unleash a strong strike with minimum danger.

squad makeup: Consider the general makeup of your squad before joining a match. A well-rounded squad with a mix of offensive, defensive, and support hunters is generally more successful than a team formed entirely of damage dealers.

Practice Makes Perfect: Honing Your Skills for Arena Domination

The route to mastery needs effort and practice. Here are some strategies to develop your talents and become an unstoppable force on the battlefield:

Utilize the Practice Arena: The practice arena is an essential tool for experimenting with new methods, practicing aiming with various weapons, and trying out ability combinations with partners. Use this place to develop your abilities before entering into competitive bouts.

Observe Skilled Players: Watch replays of high-level players, especially those who specialize in your chosen hunter. Analyze their movement patterns, ability utilization, and general strategic approach to gather vital knowledge.

Learn from Your Mistakes: Analyze your performance after each match, noting areas where you struggled or made errors. Use this knowledge to adapt your strategy and concentrate on progress in upcoming bouts.

Adaptability is Key: The Evolving Arena

The terrain of Star Wars Hunters is continuously expanding, with new hunters, weaponry, and maps being launched periodically. Here's how to remain ahead of the curve:

Stay Updated: Keep yourself updated about new content additions via official sources including developer updates, patch notes, and community forums. Understanding the changes to the game will help you to alter your strategy properly.

Embrace New Tactics: Don't be hesitant to experiment with new tactics and squad compositions as the game progresses. What worked yesterday may not be as successful today, so be adaptable and change your strategy depending on the current situation.

Sharpen Your Skills Continuously: The quest to mastery is never-ending. Constantly seek to enhance your aiming, mobility, and strategic thinking. The more you train and polish your talents, the more dominating you will become in the arenas.

Conclusion: The Arena Awaits

The arenas are your proving grounds, hunter. By learning the art of battle, employing cover and placement tactically, and working efficiently with your squad, you'll convert from a beginner hunter into a legend. Remember, the route to mastery involves effort, practice, and a willingness to adapt. So, go out, polish your abilities, and become the uncontested champion of the Star Wars Hunters arenas!

CONCLUSION

Welcome back, hunter! You've gone on an extraordinary trip through the Star Wars Hunters experience. This thorough book has prepared you with the information and methods to not only survive in the arenas but to conquer them. From mastering your weapons and skills to expressing yourself via personalization and planning for team triumph, you now possess the tools to become a famous hunter.

Beyond the Basics: The Ongoing Evolution of Star Wars Hunters

The universe of Star Wars Hunters is a dynamic, breathing organism continually changing with new material and upgrades. Here's how you remain ahead of the curve and continue to succeed in an ever-changing environment:

Embrace the Journey: The route to mastery is a constant learning process. New hunters, weapons, skills, areas, and game types will be launched throughout time, keeping the gaming experience new and difficult. Approach these additions with eagerness and a readiness to learn and adapt.

Engage with the Community: The Star Wars Hunters community is a dynamic area filled with dedicated gamers. Utilize online forums, social media groups, and in-game chat capabilities to interact with other hunters, exchange techniques, debate the newest developments, and join in friendly competition.

Seek Knowledge and Inspiration: Watch broadcasts and videos from content artists that specialize in Star Wars Hunters. Learn from their gameplay, evaluate their techniques, and gather vital ideas to better your own talents. Remember, there's always something new to learn, even from the most experienced players.

The Art of Sportsmanship: A Legacy of Honor

While success is a good aim, it's how you get it that defines your character as a hunter. Here are some concepts to adopt for a more pleasant and fun gaming experience for yourself and your fellow hunters:

Respect Your Opponents: Every hunter, regardless of skill level, deserves respect. Celebrate triumphs with humility and provide words of encouragement to those you defeat. A kind victor gets the respect of the community.

Embrace Teamwork: Remember, Star Wars Hunters is a team-based game. Communicate effectively with your coworkers, prioritize their well-being, and enjoy triumphs as a unit. Strong collaboration is not only about winning; it's about promoting camaraderie and establishing strong connections within the community.

Learn from Losses: Even the most expert hunters experience defeat. Analyze your defeats honestly, discover areas for development, and utilize them as stepping stones on your journey to mastery. A optimistic attitude and a willingness to learn from errors are crucial attributes of a great winner.

The Legacy You Leave Behind

As you create your course through the arenas, remember that your deeds leave a lasting imprint. Will you be recognized as a tough opponent, a brilliant strategist, or a gracious victor? The option is yours, hunter. Strive to create a good influence on the Star Wars Hunters community, encouraging others with your abilities and sportsmanship.

The Force is With You

The cosmos awaits, hunter. With the information and methods gathered from this book, you are now well-equipped to dominate the arenas and make your imprint on the Star Wars Hunters world. May the Force be with you on your road to legendary greatness.

PART 4

APPENDICES & RESOURCES

Appendix A: Hunter Reference Guide (Detailed Stats and Ability Breakdowns)

Welcome, hunters! This detailed guide digs deep into the arsenals of each playable character in Star Wars Hunters. Here, you'll discover extensive summaries of their stats, skills, and playstyle considerations to help you master every hunter and conquer the arenas.

Hunter Statistics:

Each hunter contains distinct basic statistics that determine their strengths and limitations. This information is vital for understanding a hunter's function on the battlefield:

Health: This shows the hunter's maximum hit points. Hunters with high health are more resilient, while those with lesser health excel in rapid mobility and offensive powers.

Shield: Some hunters possess shields that absorb harm before exhausting their health. Shields may be vital for defensive playstyles.

Movement Speed: This controls how swiftly a hunter can cross the battlefield. Fast hunters excel in flanking tactics and escaping danger, whereas slower hunters depend on placement and concealment.

Energy Recharge: This attribute impacts how fast a hunter regains energy needed to trigger their powers. Hunters with quicker energy recharge may deploy skills more often.

Ability Breakdowns:

Each hunter boasts three distinct talents that dictate their strategic choices. Here's a breakdown of the information you'll discover for each ability:

Ability Name: A clear and succinct term for the ability.

Ability Type: This categorizes the ability as Offensive, Defensive, or Utility, offering a basic notion of its use.

Description: A full description of the ability's effects, including damage done (offensive), amount of healing delivered (defensive), or special utility effects (e.g., stuns, speed boosts).

Cooldown Timer: The time it takes for an ability to recharge after being utilized. Managing cooldowns efficiently is crucial for sustaining a continual flow of tactical choices in combat.

region of Effect (AoE): This specifies whether the ability impacts a certain region surrounding the hunter, affecting many foes or friends within range.

Upgrade Path: Each skill may be improved using in-game credits. This section describes the consequences of each upgrade level, showing higher damage output, prolonged durations, or other functionality for your skills.

Hunter Playstyle Considerations:

Beyond numbers and skills, this article gives insights on each hunter's preferred playstyle:

Offensive Powerhouses: These hunters excel in dealing great damage and eliminating foes swiftly. They generally demand strong aim and aggressive techniques.

Defensive Bulwarks: These hunters emphasize defending themselves and their comrades. They employ shields, healing skills, and clever placement to help their squad.

Tactical Specialists: These hunters possess special utility skills that may control adversary movement, disrupt opposing strategy, or give strategic bonuses for their teammates. They depend on sophisticated methods and timing to maximize their influence.

Utilizing the Hunter Reference Guide:

To best use this tutorial, take these steps:

1. Choose Your Hunter: Identify the hunter you desire to learn more about.

2. Review Stats: Analyze their basic data to determine their strengths and limitations.

3. Deep Dive into Abilities: Read the comprehensive breakdowns of each ability, paying special attention to cooldowns, AoE effects, and upgrade pathways.

4. Consider Playstyle: Understand the hunter's optimal role on the battlefield, whether it's aggressive offensive, robust defense, or tactical usefulness.

This Hunter Reference Guide is a fantastic resource for mastering every character in Star Wars Hunters. Utilize it properly, and you'll be well on your way to becoming a legend in the arena!

Appendix B: Crafting Material Guide (How to Obtain and Use)

Welcome, resourceful hunters! The arenas are not only about fighting prowess; they also reward your ability to obtain and use precious manufacturing materials. This article discusses the numerous crafting materials available in Star Wars Hunters and how to utilize them to strengthen your hunter's armament.

Types of Crafting Materials:

There are three basic kinds of crafting materials in Star Wars Hunters:

Common Materials: These are widely acquired via different gaming activities, such as finishing matches and engaging in daily challenges. Common materials are utilized for basic upgrades and weapon modifications.

Uncommon Materials: These are rarer than common materials and are often gained via more demanding activities, such as ranking high in competitive matches or completing special events. Uncommon resources are utilized for more complex upgrades and weapon modifications.

Rare Materials: These are the most hardest to get, frequently reserved for high-level prizes and particular in-game events. Rare resources are utilized for constructing the most potent upgrades and special weapon modifications.

Obtaining Crafting Materials:

Here's a rundown of how to get different ...making ingredients in Star Wars Hunters:

Match Completion: Every match you finish, regardless of success or failure, provides you with a little number of common resources. Consistency is crucial to establishing a continuous supply.

Daily Challenges: Daily challenges give chances to gain more common and unusual resources. These challenges often include fulfilling specific goals inside matches, such as eliminating a certain number of foes with a certain weapon or seizing objectives in objective-based game variants.

Weekly Challenges: Similar to daily challenges, weekly challenges provide more challenging goals and bigger prizes, including uncommon and even rare resources. These challenges can include winning a given number of matches with a specific hunter or earning a high rating in a particular game mode.

Ranked Play: As you climb the rankings in competitive play, your prizes rise, allowing a chance to gain uncommon and even rare resources depending on your performance.

unique Events: Limited-time events typically feature crafting materials as prizes for accomplishing event-specific tasks or playing in unique game modes. These occurrences may be a rich source of uncommon and rare items.

Using Crafting Materials:

Crafting resources are used to enhance several components of your hunter's arsenal:

Weapon Upgrades: Crafting resources may be used to upgrade weapon statistics, such as increasing damage output, enhancing accuracy, or raising firing rate.

Ability Upgrades: You may employ resources to enhance your hunter's skills, unlocking extra effects, lowering cooldowns, or increasing durations of certain abilities.

Crafting Weapon modifications: Certain crafting materials may be utilized to build unique weapon modifications that modify the functioning of your weapons. These modifications may give numerous advantages, such as enhancing elemental damage, delivering extra effects on critical strikes, or increasing magazine capacity.

Optimizing Material Usage:

Here are some strategies to optimize your utilization of crafting materials:

Prioritize Upgrades: Focus on enhancing the characteristics of your hunter that best fit your playstyle. If you like aggressive tactics, prioritize weapon improvements. If you love a supporting position, concentrate on ability enhancements.

Plan for the Future: Consider potential content releases and new hunts you could unlock. Save some of your rarer resources for possible improvements to future additions to your team.

Utilize Crafting Guides: Online resources and community forums typically give crafting guidelines that indicate best upgrading pathways for various hunts and weapon kinds. Utilize these resources to guarantee you're utilizing your supplies effectively.

Crafting materials are the essence of customization and optimization in Star Wars Hunters. By meticulously obtaining them and deploying them correctly, you'll guarantee your hunter's armament stays formidable and adaptive to the ever-evolving challenges of the arenas!

Appendix C: Glossary of Terms

Welcome, eager hunters! Mastering the venues needs not only fighting skill but also a thorough understanding of the vocabulary employed in Star Wars Hunters. This dictionary acts as a helpful reference tool for crucial terminology you'll meet along your adventure.

General Terms:

Hunter: A playable character in Star Wars Hunters, each with distinct skills and playstyles.

Arena: The battlefields where hunters engage in different game types.

Match: An particular instance of gaming when hunters compete to fulfill certain goals.

Ability: A unique ability employed by each hunter, delivering attacking, defensive, or utility advantages.

Upgrade: An upgrade to a hunter's skills, weaponry, or statistics via the use of crafting resources.

Weapon Mod: An attachment that improves a weapon's functioning, delivering unique effects or extra stats.

Cooldown: The time it takes for an ability to recharge after being utilized.

region of Effect (AoE): An ability that influences a defined region surrounding the hunter, impacting many foes or friends within range.

Game Mode Terms:

seize the Flag: A game mode where teams compete to seize and hold the enemy team's flag.

Droid Rush: A game mode where teams compete to gather and place droids into predefined zones.

Payload: A game mode where teams battle to transport or protect a moving payload across the map.

Domination: A game mode where teams seize and maintain control points to win points and achieve victory.

Ranked Play: A competitive mode where players fight for rank by attaining high placements in matches.

Other Important Terms:

Meta: The current prevailing methods and tactics adopted by high-level players in the game.

Emote: An emote lets your hunter to convey emotions or conduct activities using animations.

Victory posture: A joyful posture your hunter may execute after earning victory in a competition.

Customization: The process of modifying your hunter's look with skins, weapon wraps, and other cosmetics.

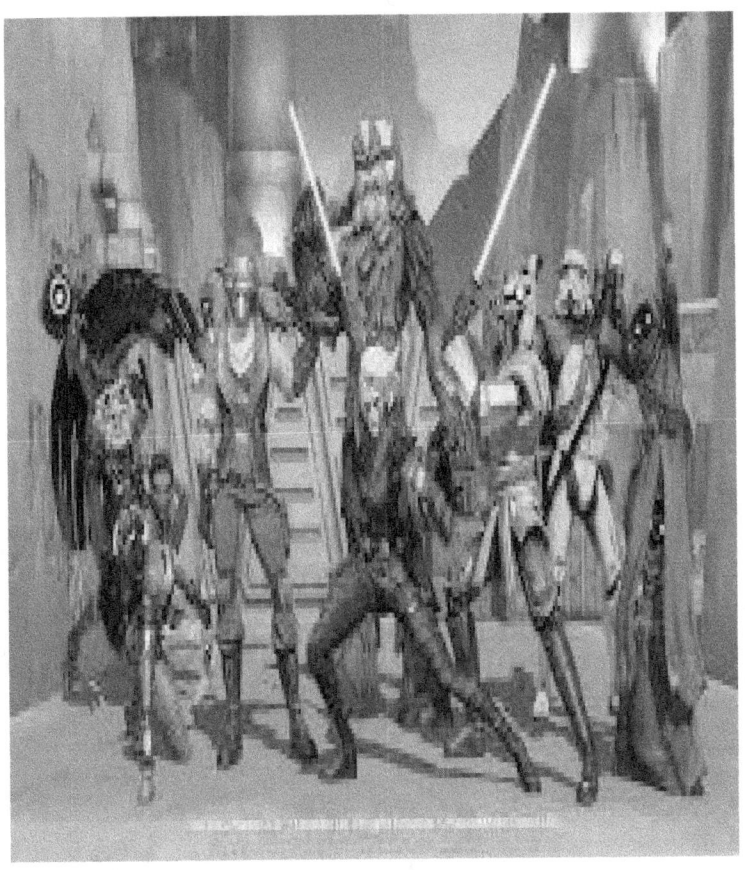